The Hunting Debate

Aiming at the Issues

Trudy J. Hanmer

Enslow Publishers, Inc.

40 Industrial Road   PO Box 38
Box 398   Aldershot
Berkeley Heights, NJ 07922 Hants GU12 6BP
USA   UK

http://www.enslow.com

For Tasia, Sloan and Hanna,
whose grandpa was a hunter

Library of Congress Cataloging-in-Publication Data

Hanmer, Trudy J.
 The hunting debate: aiming at the issues / Trudy J. Hanmer
  p. cm. — (Issues in focus)
 Includes bibliographical references and index.
 Summary: Examines both sides of the debate over whether
recreational hunting is a cruel practice or a legitimate sport,
discussing such aspects as gun control, animal population control,
and the traditional nature of the activity.
  ISBN 0-7660-1110-0
 1. Hunting—Moral and ethical aspects—Juvenile literature.
[1. Hunting—Moral and ethical aspects.] I. Title. II. Series:
Issues in Focus (Hillside, N.J.)
SK14.3H25 1999
179'.3—dc21   98-54590
                CIP

Printed in the United States of America

10 9 8 7 6 5 4 3 2

To Our Readers:
All Internet addresses in this book were active and appropriate when
we went to press. Any comments or suggestions can be sent by e-mail
to comments@enslow.com or to the address on the back cover.

Illustration Credits: © Corel Corporation, pp. 10, 13, 26, 28,
35, 46, 61, 65, 67, 75, 77, 80, 101; Library of Congress,
p. 92; Sagamore Hill National Historic Site, National Park
Service, Oyster Bay, New York, p. 43; Texas State Library &
Archives Commission, pp. 41, 44; Trudy J. Hanmer, pp. 18, 20,
23, 33, 49, 51, 63, 69, 87, 88, 95.

Cover Illustration: © Corel Corporation

Contents

1

A Dual Image—
Heroes and
Villains

*The game seemed to him to be two
different animals. On the chase it was the
quarry. He wanted only to see it fall. . . .
When it lay dead and bleeding, he was sickened and sorry. . . . Then when it was cut
into portions . . . his mouth watered at its
goodness. He wondered by what alchemy it
was changed so that what sickened him one
hour, maddened him with hunger the next.
It seemed as if there were either two different animals or two different boys.*
—Marjorie Kinnan Rawlings,
The Yearling

This passage from the classic novel *The
Yearling* captures the central conflict
between hunters and those who oppose
hunting. Sometimes, this conflict can exist

within one person, as in the case of the young hero of *The Yearling.* Even an experienced hunter can feel remorse and sadness at the death of an animal. Yet the rewards for killing the animal—the basic survival provided by capturing food or the luxury of a delicious meal—may make the killing justifiable and even pleasurable. For people opposed to hunting, however, there is rarely any justification for hunting and killing an animal.

The controversy over hunting has become particularly heated in the United States at the beginning of the twenty-first century. Arguments for and against hunting are complex and have become intertwined with a number of other issues such as animal rights, the right to bear arms and gun control, conservation, and ecology. Although there are some people in the world who must still hunt to survive—for example, Inuit tribes living above the Arctic Circle—this is no longer the case for people living in modern, urbanized America. Practically no one in the United States of America must hunt to survive.

Animals Killed Annually

Two hundred million animals are legally killed by hunters each year in the United States. Whereas the majority of American hunters pursue deer, hunters also kill doves, rabbits, squirrels, quail, pheasants, ducks, geese, elk, and black bear. Hunters argue that people cannot live unless other living things die, and unless we are vegetarians, our food needs must depend on the deaths of animals.

In fact, hunters do not kill the majority of animals in the United States each year. Each year, the food industry kills 35 million cattle, 6 million sheep, 85 million pigs, 400 million chickens, and 300 million turkeys to supply food for American families. Even the production of grains and vegetables can be destructive to animal life. The intensive cultivation used by modern agriculture destroys millions of small mammals—for example, field mice and rabbits. Often these animals are killed directly when they or their nests are run over by large farm machinery. They also die when large agricultural projects convert the land that provides their habitats into land for cultivation. Some ecologists believe that the destruction of habitat for large-scale agriculture, housing developments, and shopping malls threatens many more animals than does the sport of hunting.

Few people question the threat that humans pose to animals of all kinds. However, the idea that people need to hunt animals is very controversial.

More than 15 million Americans hunt every year. They choose to do so for a variety of reasons, only one of which is to provide food for themselves and their families. Although they may prefer the taste of fresh game or enjoy decreasing the family's meat bill, they do not depend on hunting for survival. Hunters also hunt for recreation. Their enjoyment comes from both being outdoors and mastering the skills necessary to track game successfully and shoot accurately. Many hunters also value the camaraderie that comes from sharing a pastime with fellow hunters; others just like the challenge of hunting a trophy animal.

Why People Oppose Hunting

A growing number of people today actively oppose hunting. They are particularly critical of recreational or sport hunting. To these antihunters, hunting purely for sport seems especially cruel. Polls taken in the 1990s indicate that whereas an overwhelming majority of Americans, as many as 80 percent, approve of hunting for meat, a sizable majority of 60 percent disapprove of hunting for sport.

People who actively oppose hunting believe that deliberately killing wild animals is wrong and should be stopped. In one recent poll, a third of the people interviewed who opposed hunting indicated that they favored a ban on all hunting. There are approximately 10 million Americans who actively oppose all hunting. Their numbers are growing, and often they belong to one of several animal rights organizations that share the abolition of hunting as a primary goal.

Pros and Cons of Hunting

Antihunting advocates view hunters as violent and the killing of animals as ecologically damaging. They believe that although hunting may once have been a necessary human activity, today it is an unnecessary part of life in a technological society. A popular antihunting bumper sticker reads, "I Support the Right to Arm Bears." Animal rights activists, who most often oppose hunting, base their beliefs on the principle that animals have rights, including the right not to be killed.

Hunters counter this argument by asserting that people are animals among many others and that it is part of the natural order for humans to kill other animals. Hunters question the idea that it is considered immoral for the human animal to kill other animals, but considered natural when one wild animal kills another. Recalling his childhood growing up near a forest, one hunter recalled, "Often we saw how mink would kill muskrats, ripping their throats open and eating just the choice parts of the body. Foxes caught mice, pike swallowed smaller fish, ospreys dropped out of the sky and caught fish hiding under lily pads, herons speared fish, and great horned owls swooped down and caught rabbits, all within a hundred feet of my bedroom."[1]

Hunters are also quick to point out that hunters began the modern conservation movement in the United States. Hunting organizations have worked as hard as any other group of Americans to preserve wildlife habitats.

As more and more land in the United States is put to use by human beings, the contact between wild animals and humans has grown more frequent. Moose are now spotted frequently along major roads in Vermont and Maine.[2] (In 1992, there were 197 moose-car collisions in Vermont alone.) Mountain lions pose a real threat to joggers in California, and alligators are frequent but unwanted visitors to Florida golf courses. Coyotes are responsible for eating pets in Arizona suburbs. Up and down the

Moose, once almost extinct in the northeastern United States, have become increasingly common. Moose have been sighted within residential areas in New York State.

East Coast, homeowners and suburban gardeners plot ways to keep deer from eating their bushes, trees, and flowers.

Habitat Conservation and Wildlife Management

It is clear that wild animals are seen more and more frequently in residential areas due to human greed for more and more land. Hunters have opposed the destruction of wildlife habitat that results from urban and suburban growth. They have, in fact, supported the establishment of millions of acres of publicly protected wildlife refuge. Some hunters actively create private wildlife sanctuaries. All hunters contribute to the government's protection of wildlife areas through the purchase of hunting and fishing licenses and permits and by paying special taxes on the weapons, ammunition, and equipment used for hunting. Virtually all of this revenue is used to support state and federal wildlife management programs. Hunters are also quick to mention that none of the major conservation organizations in the United States opposes hunting.

Hunters also argue that, by its very nature, hunting provides valuable conservation services because it helps limit the animal population. Because hunting is regulated by season and quotas, wildlife biologists can control the wild animal population in any given area. They argue that hunting is an effective—and humane—method of population control. If the deer population becomes too large in a certain area because of an abundance of food, for example, the increased number of deer may starve later when the food supply becomes scarce.

Starving is a slow and painful way to die compared with death as the result of a bullet or arrow fired by a skilled hunter. If the hunter strikes the animal in the targeted heart/lungs region, death can occur in less than thirty seconds. Starvation can take weeks. On the other hand, antihunters argue that any violent death, no matter how quickly carried out, is cruel and unnecessary. "There is no such thing as a little death,"[3] commented writer T. H. Watkins.

Opponents of hunting disapprove of its use as a

wildlife management tool. Although critics of hunting do not dispute the fact that hunting fees have been used to pay for wildlife management programs, they believe that the programs funded in this way have focused too exclusively on wild game animals that are prized by hunters. In other words, such programs primarily service the needs of hunters rather than of animals. Critics argue that the same money could be used for alternative methods of population control—for example, programs to neuter deer—that would help the animals, but not the hunters. Hunting opponents also believe that because hunters provide these funds, they have too much influence on those who carry out the wildlife programs. Too many game wardens and wildlife biologists, they believe, are hunters themselves, who spend time and resources to preserve the best hunting conditions, rather than searching for other ways to manage all wildlife.

Another reason hunting survives, its opponents point out, is that hunting is big business. In 1991, 14 million hunters spent $12.3 billion in support of their sport, an average of nearly $900 per person. Critics of hunting deplore the new technology available to hunters that allow them to "outsmart" the animals they seek. The equipment includes high-velocity rifles; infrared glasses; biologically sophisticated, man-made animal scents; and calls. Hunting critics consider these aids to be the worst examples of how humankind preys on innocent wildlife. Some states have, in fact, outlawed the use of many of these devices.

Hunters argue that they spend far more time than

Hunting is big business. A hunter spends approximately nine hundred dollars a year on the sport for equipment and clothing.

their opponents do in the woods learning the ways of animals. They maintain that hunting is a physically challenging sport that heightens one's awareness of animals and their habitats. Hunters frequently cite the teachings of native peoples who believed that hunting brought humans into spiritual contact with their prey. American Indian shamans believed that there was interspecies communication between the hunter and the hunted. These religious leaders claimed that animals "are willing to let humans kill some of their kind for food as long as they agree to care for the rest of the species."[4]

Gun Control and Hunting

Hunting is connected to the issue of gun control. Gun control advocates argue that hunting is dangerous and that both hunters and innocent human bystanders who are nonhunters are killed each year by hunters' bullets. They also argue that guns in homes, while intended for hunting, too often become human murder weapons. When two preteen boys from Jonesboro, Arkansas, murdered several of their classmates, the unavoidable reality was that they knew guns and how to use them because they had been taught to hunt at an early age. The guns were owned by one boy's grandfather, who was a hunter. Hunters respond that this tragedy, like others, is unavoidable in a world where some people—and some animals—are bad and do evil things. They argue that no one in the boys' families taught them that killing people was good. In fact, the boys broke into their grandfather's house and stole the guns. Hunters mourn the deaths of the schoolgirls as a senseless, tragic act, but not one that should be laid at the feet of hunting—any more than a death caused by a speeding automobile should be blamed on trained sportscar racers.

In 1999, following the massacre of twelve students and one teacher in Littleton, Colorado, by two students who then killed themselves, President Bill Clinton proposed new gun control legislation. Some of the items in Clinton's proposal included limiting handgun sales to one per month to any one person, restoring a waiting period before any handgun purchase, raising the minimum age for legal possession of a handgun to twenty-one from eighteen, and banning a minor's possession of semiautomatic assault rifles.

Deciding Whether or Not to Hunt

Whether or not to hunt is a decision some young people will face personally, although the percentage of young people choosing to hunt has declined annually. For most, however, their opinions about hunting will involve public policy, rather than personal behavior. The choice to support or oppose hunting in modern American society may soon appear on the ballot. During the 1990s, voters in California, Colorado, Alaska, and a number of other states have already limited certain types of hunting. It is likely that today's students will be asked, as tomorrow's voters, to cast a vote for or against hunting. This book will frame the issues surrounding hunting and provide information that may help one make this decision if and when the time comes.

2

Hunting: Who, What, and How?

And when some of my friends have asked me anxiously about their boys, whether they should let them hunt, I have answered yes—remembering that it was one of the best parts of my education—make them hunters.

—Henry David Thoreau

It's preposterous that every year less than 7 percent of the population turns the skies into shooting galleries. . . .

—Joy Williams,
Anti-Hunting Activist

Although hunters represent a small percentage of the American population, their numbers are significant. Between 15 and 20 million people over the age of sixteen hunt. Who are they? Why do they hunt? What do they hunt, and how do they do it? Some of the answers to these questions highlight the differences of opinion between those who support hunting and those who oppose it.

A Hunter's Profile

At the end of World War II, approximately 25 percent of American men aged sixteen or older were legal hunters, meaning that they had purchased a hunting license. Although some women hunted during that period, their numbers were insignificant. By 1991, the percentage of Americans who hunted had dropped to 7.4 percent, but 11 percent of these hunters were women. Today, the total number of hunters is only slightly smaller than the number of people who play tennis, golf, or softball. In those other sports, the percentage of men to women is far higher even than in hunting, which is usually identified as a male sport.

People who do not hunt may think of hunters as uneducated and rural, but the average hunter is a white male with some college education who earns, on the average, $43,000 a year. On the average, these hunters hunt seven to ten days a year and limit their hunting to within fifty miles of their home.

American hunters overwhelmingly seek deer as their preferred prey. Ten out of fourteen hunting licenses are purchased by hunters whose goal is to kill a deer. Most hunters use rifles or shotguns, but one third of all hunters use bows and arrows. Nearly

The average hunter is a white male with slightly more college education than the average American. All of the hunters in this picture, members of a hunting camp, are doctors, lawyers, bankers, and other professional businessmen.

half of all hunters do not own a single handgun, the least common weapon used in hunting.

The state with the fewest hunters is California. Since the late 1960s, California has seen a steady decline in the percentage of citizens who hunt. The anti-Vietnam War movement, increasing urbanization and land development, and growing interest in vegetarianism, animal rights, and gun control have contributed to the decline of hunting in the nation's most populous state. During the 1990s, less than one percent of the population, or about four hundred thousand Californians, purchased hunting licenses each year.

At the other end of the spectrum, Arkansas has the largest percentage of hunters. In 1993, 50 percent of the state's population bought hunting licenses. President Bill Clinton, probably the most famous hunter from Arkansas, said, "I can still remember the first time I pulled a trigger on a .410 shotgun....[Hunting] is a part of the culture of a big part of America."[1] The president appreciates the tradition of hunting. However, those who oppose hunting point out that among the recent rash of tragic schoolyard shootings, the largest number have occurred in Arkansas, where children have the greatest chance in the nation of living in a house where guns are present.

Reasons for Hunting

Hunters can be divided into three categories: meat hunters, recreational or sport hunters, and nature hunters.[2] Meat hunters are the most numerous and make up nearly half the hunting population. They hunt strictly to provide food for themselves and their families. They choose fresh game over processed meat for its nutritional value. Recreational hunters account for 38 percent of all hunters. They may or may not eat the meat from the animals they kill; for them, the hunting experience is far more important than either killing or procuring food. The smallest group is composed of nature hunters, people who view hunting as a sacred or spiritual act. Psychologist Erich Fromm described nature hunters in this way: "In the act of hunting, a man becomes, however briefly, part of nature again. He returns to the natural state [and] becomes one with the animal."[3]

When they were asked why they hunted, hunters gave four reasons: to socialize with people who share a common interest; to escape from the pressures of urban living; to get away from the routine of the workplace; and to procure food. Only 10 percent of hunters stated that they did it to capture a trophy

Most hunters list companionship as one of their primary reasons for hunting.

animal for the record books or to display on their den walls.[4]

Being out in the woods with a group of friends ranks high on the list of the reasons people hunt. One hunter recalled the boyhood thrill of going to a local hunting spot called Hinkel's Woods, where he and his friends sought rabbits and other small game. "Going to Hinkel's was like going to hunting camp. Throwing up a lean-to and building a fire in front of it, and stacking the rifles against a tree, and roasting meat on sticks, and smelling wood smoke, and being away for a while from family and other friends," was the best part of hunting for him as a boy.[5]

Most adult hunters started hunting as children accompanying their parents, usually their fathers. Russell Chatham had wonderful memories of hunting with his father:

> My recollections of hunting in those formative years concern the smell of sage and tocalote, the forlorn soft sound of the mourning dove in the distance . . . breezes rattling the dry oak leaves . . . the afternoon sun diffused through the sycamores, the presence of my father just beside me or else whistling his familiar whistle behind a stand of trees.[6]

Many women also have good memories of childhood experiences hunting with their fathers. Congresswoman Blanche Lambert (Democrat, Arkansas) is a member of the Congressional Sportsmen's Congress. She has written,

> Bracing against the pre-dawn chill in a duck blind with my father is one of my most vivid memories

of growing up in East Arkansas. Similar mental snapshots have been created across our nation for centuries as parents have introduced their children to the beauty of our wildlife through hunting and fishing.[7]

Like most hunters, Representative Lambert prizes the time she spends outdoors as one of the great benefits of hunting.

Stages of Hunting

Three psychologists at the University of Wisconsin have identified five stages that hunters go through as they develop from adolescence to adulthood.[8] First is the shooter stage, when shooting a gun is the best thing about hunting. Thomas McIntyre, a writer and hunter, recalled that he "was four, I guess, when my dad first held [his] rifle up to my shoulder and passed on his knowledge of it to me."[9] His father showed him how to shoot, and "when I fired that first shot, the sound was like the ripping of some thick fabric, and I was irreparably embarked on something that would occupy the rest of my life."[10]

The second stage is the "limiting out stage," when the quantity of animals taken appears to be the most important facet of the hunt. The boastful Davy Crockett claimed once to have killed one hundred bears in a year, as though the sheer quantity of what he had killed demonstrated his hunting superiority. Apparently some hunters, no matter how experienced, ever progress beyond this stage. At the turn of the century, aristocratic hunters such as England's Prince of Wales were proud of the quantity of game

Hunters claim it is good for young people to learn to hunt with their parents, but many gun control advocates maintain that hunting encourages violence and leads to childhood accidents and deaths.

they shot. On December 18, 1913, shortly before he became King George V, the Prince of Wales and his friends shot nearly four thousand pheasants in a single day.

Third is the trophy stage. At this point, the size of each animal shot is more important than shooting a quantity of animals. Professional trophy hunters never leave this stage. They spend a great deal of time and money chasing the biggest specimens they can find. They search for the heaviest elk or the deer with the most points on its antlers in order to see their names in the record books. Ironically, most hunters who successfully shoot trophy animals do so somewhat spontaneously. As hunters grow older, they become more thoughtful. These are hunters who let the first, second, or third deer or elk or bear of the season pass by without a kill, in the hope that they will sight a larger, older, or more heavily antlered animal later in the season.

The fourth stage of hunting is the method stage. Hunters in this stage focus on how they hunt, and many are tempted to buy gadgets and to try new techniques. They spend weeks before hunting season poring over catalogs. They visit sports shops to test new rifles and new equipment and are convinced that the key to the perfect hunt lies in having the latest equipment. Hunters at this stage are older. They often have more money available to them to spend on their sport.

The final stage for most hunters is the sportsman stage. At this point, wrote sportsman Ted Kerasote, hunters "are satisfied merely to be outside and give up control of the world."[11] Jim Milsna, an experienced hunter who went for twenty seasons without ever shooting a deer, had clearly reached the sportsman stage. He commented on his reasons for continuing to hunt without the satisfaction of bringing home a deer: "Obviously, I'm doing it not so much for the game, but because I enjoy hunting, and the camaraderie that goes with it, and the challenge, and the venison [deer meat], if we get any. But the biggest part of all is just being out there, the sheer pleasure of sitting in the woods, me and nature together."[12] The more quickly a hunter reaches this final stage, the more likely he or she is to have spent time with parents who are thoughtful, careful hunters.

Different Kinds of Hunting

There are almost as many ways to hunt as there are hunters. Every hunter has his or her favorite weapons, place to hunt, kind of prey to hunt, and method of hunting. Hunting rules and laws also vary from state to state.

Some hunters hunt on foot, some from all-terrain vehicles, some on horseback. Where it is legal to do so, many hunters use dogs to help them track animals. Hunters use rifles, shotguns, muzzle-loaders, or bow and arrow. Most use rifles, and there are many different brands and calibers of rifles they can use. Some hunters hunt on private land, others on public hunting grounds or managed animal preserves. While most hunt near home, others fly or drive hundreds or

There are many types of weapons a hunter can use. Some prefer the challenge of bow and arrow.

even thousands of miles in order to hunt unusual exotic game, to gain the expertise of certain guides, or to experience special geographic areas.

Hunting Regulations

What, when, and how a person can hunt are regulated by state laws. Every state has different regulations, and each state requires that hunters purchase permits and licenses that apply only to that state. Each state produces a book of regulations detailing the laws for that state, and most states have developed Web sites that allow people to view online the hunting laws for that state.

Most states have multiple hunting seasons. Thus, a state may have different seasons for hunting turkey, bear, deer, fox, and wildfowl. In fact, states usually issue separate regulations for every animal that can be hunted legally. Often these seasons overlap, because most legal hunting is done in the fall. If there are no restrictions on when an animal can be hunted—for example, bobcats and coyotes in Alabama—the animal is said to have an "open season all year around." For other animals that are protected against hunting, there is "no season" at any time. For example, there is no season on alligators or on owls in any state.

Hunting regulations in most states vary according to the weapons that are used, and they generally specify the number of animals that can be taken by any one hunter. This number is called a bag limit. In some states, hunters are limited to one or two deer per season. In others, the bag limit can be as many as one deer per day during the legal season. Hunting regulations may vary from county to county within a state.

In North America, it is most common for animals of all kinds to follow a cycle in which they give birth in the spring and spend much of the summer months stocking up on food to survive during the winter months when food is scarce. Spring hunting, although legal in some areas for some species, is regarded by opponents of hunting as the cruelest time to hunt.

Spring hunting often means that female animals who are taken by a hunter leave behind their young. These orphans almost always die without their mothers to protect them.

Loons, like the one pictured, are protected from hunting in most states.

Some hunting is regulated by law to a specific time of day. In New York State, for example, wild turkey can be hunted only before noon. In Alabama during dove season, mourning doves can only be hunted from noon until sunset.

Regulation of Weapons

Hunting weapons are also regulated. Most hunters use rifles or shotguns, but some use muzzle-loaders, a traditional rifle that requires reloading after each shot. Still others choose bow and arrow. In most states, each of these types of weapons has a different season. Alabama, for example, regulates its deer season according to shotgun, bow and arrow, spear, and rifle use.

Some opponents of hunting have directed their activity at limiting certain weapons or methods of hunting. While they may not oppose all hunting, they believe certain types of hunting are particularly cruel. During the 1990s, animal rights groups have been responsible for the passage of numerous laws limiting the kinds of weapons that hunters may use. In 1994, Oregon, California, and Colorado banned the use of hounds to hunt bear. Arizona banned the use of traps on state land. Colorado has banned snaring, trapping, and poisoning as ways of killing mountain lions. Idaho, Michigan, and Washington have passed laws banning baiting and hounding of bear. Washington also banned the hounding of lynx, cougar, and bobcat, and Massachusetts banned the leghold trapping of bear and bobcat.

Licensing and Charges: Public and Private Fees

To hunt legally in the United States, it is necessary to purchase a license. The license is issued for a specific time length and allows the pursuit of a specific animal or animals. Both the government and private landowners can charge people extra fees to hunt specialized animals or to take part in special hunts. These hunts are used to reduce the population of common animals or to provide hunters with special, controlled opportunities to capture certain animals.

In the United States, there are seven thousand

commercial shooting preserves in which animals are restrained and bred solely for hunting. Sportswriter Ted Williams described one such preserve in Massachusetts where for eight dollars per bird, hunters, positioned on shooting towers, can fire away at these birds. This kind of hunting is particularly distressing to animal rights activists. Hunters who stalk their game through the wilderness are also often critical of those who trap helpless animals and shoot them for profit.

Other kinds of legal hunting, some promoted by state governments, have been criticized by hunters and nonhunters alike. When the elk population in Wyoming outgrew the carrying capacity of the wildlife refuge, the state issued special permits allowing hunters to hunt elk in the area. Because the elk were numerous and were used to feeding peacefully in the refuge, locating them was not a challenge. As one elk hunter wrote, "Hunting elk from horseback or on foot, up in the mountains, is one thing, and hunting elk from a pickup parked along the tarmac is another—even in the eyes of a lot of meat-eating Wyomingites."[13]

Hunting Clubs

Most hunters choose to hunt in groups. Often this means belonging to a hunting club. Since the late nineteenth century, when Theodore Roosevelt and a group of his wealthy friends founded the Boone and Crockett Club to preserve hunting, hunting clubs and camps have been an important part of the ritual of the sport.

One of the advantages of a hunting club is that such clubs generally own acres of wilderness where the members can hunt. Often they employ caretakers who serve as guides. Because they live at the camp year-round, they can watch the habits of the animals and lead the hunters to their quarry's favorite feeding spots. Hunting clubs also check to make sure their members have purchased the appropriate licenses and do not allow their members to hunt unless they are properly licensed.

For those who oppose hunting, the hunting club often symbolizes the worst aspects of the sport. Frequently, these clubs are portrayed as males-only strongholds where too much alcohol is consumed, sexist jokes are told, and violence against animals is celebrated by the numerous stuffed heads, antlers, and pelts adorning the walls. This image is actually very much at odds with the reality of hunting camps such as the Boone and Crockett Club, with its dual emphasis on conservation and hunting.

The Variety of Game Animals

There are more than 1,100 species of animals in the United States today. Only 145 of these are game animals that are legally hunted by humans. On the average, hunters legally kill 50 million mourning doves, 28 million quail, 25 million rabbits, 22 million squirrels, 20 million pheasant, 6 million ruffed grouse and 5.2 million ducks. Although they kill only 4 million white-tailed deer, these are their most common prey. In addition, hunters bag geese, chukar partridge, mule deer, wild turkey, coyote, pronghorn antelope, elk, black bear, brown bear, grizzly bear, caribou, moose, javelina, bighorn sheep, mountain lions, wolves, bison, musk ox, and mountain goats.

The variety of game animals is matched by the variety in their habits, migration patterns, and preferred living spaces. As hunter and naturalist Charles F. Waterman wrote, "Each game species has its own ecology."[14] As a result, most hunters concentrate on one or two animals as their prey. To learn the ways of an animal well enough to stalk and capture it requires skill and practice. Waterman also wrote that "a hunter's skills must go well beyond merely sighting and cleanly killing his game. He must be able to identify its habitat through knowledge of the appropriate vegetation and terrain. He must be woodsman enough to recognize the signs of game presence before he sees the game itself. He looks for the things his game will feed upon and the things that will feed upon his game."[15]

Hunting and the Economy

Hunting today is big business. In the 1990s, American hunters spent between $10 and $12 billion annually. Half this money was spent on guns, ammunition, camping gear, vehicles, and other equipment. Only 4 percent of the money was spent on licenses and permits. Most of the rest went toward travel, lodging, and food.

In small towns and rural areas, hunters often provide a significant source of income for small store owners.

Hunters point out that this money often provides a real economic boom to small towns when hunters arrive for the season. Hunting season is to some rural areas what the tourist season is to resort areas and what Christmas is to retailers.

Technology and Hunting

Among the advertisements in any hunting magazine will be those for clothing and a host of other technological devices that promote the idea that a successful hunt depends on up-to-date equipment. Issues of sports catalogs and hunting magazines included advertisements for the following:

> Optronics Nightblaster Gunlights, "easy to flick on when varmint is in range." (*Deer*, Fall 1997)

Game Finders, which "have adequate sensitivity to effectively penetrate wood and brush to find hidden animals." (*Deer*, Fall 1997)

Electronic calls "with 15 watt speakers for long distance capabilities" and extra call tapes for rabbits, coyotes, javelina, and "squealing rodents," among other animals. (*Deer*, Fall 1997)

Portable tree stands made of lightweight aluminum with foam cushions, a rain roof, and a camouflage covering that "allow you to hunt all day with ease." (*Deer*, Fall 1997)

"Scent Killer" that prevents human scent from spooking a deer and allows hunters "to see more deer, get closer shots." (*Hunting*, Fall 1997)

It is part of the hunting tradition, as far back as humans have hunted, to camouflage, to use better techniques, to study animals to hide scents and imitate sounds. What is new is the use of synthetic rather than natural materials to achieve these effects. As a reporter for *The New York Times* noted at the beginning of the 1997 hunting season, "Now a hunter can bag a doe with the same toys James Bond might use to down a foe."[16]

A question for both those who support and those who oppose hunting today is whether or not modern technology has made tracking animals and capturing them so easy that it is unfair. Hunters say that in spite of plentiful game in some areas, it is still very difficult to track an animal successfully and that animal cunning can never be overcome by gadgets and technology. Those who oppose hunting disagree.

Here a hunter uses a portable tree stand, one of the many types of equipment available to the hunter.

They see hunting technology as one of the evils of big business, the unfair advantage of greedy humans over innocent wildlife.

Those who oppose hunting argue that modern technology is just one more reason that hunting is no longer the time-honored tradition that it once was. Instead, they believe that hunting has become the triumph of machines over helpless animals.

Looking at some of the methods that hunters use for tracking and attracting animals highlights this controversy. Hunters often speak of and prize well-honed skills that have passed down through generations. For example, some hunters have perfected duck calls, and others can accurately mimic the sound of a wounded animal in order to bring its larger, natural predator into rifle range. A recent issue of *Outdoor Life*, a popular hunting and fishing magazine, devoted an article to crafting a turkey call from a turkey wingbone. The project required skill, knowledge of turkey anatomy, patience, and almost no cash. The author noted that the wingbone turkey call dated back to American Indians who had passed on this technique to colonial settlers. He concluded that there is "just something special about using natural materials to call in your prey."[17] In addition to instructions for building the call, there were instructions for blowing it, a skill that takes time to master.

In the same issue of this magazine, a special advertising section presented information on machine-made calls that could be purchased ready to use. The calls had names such as Screaming Hen II, Diamond Yelper, and Old Boss Hen Lite. The most expensive, Challenging Jake, could be pumped or shaken (no tricky blowing) and was described as "easier to use."[18] Given the choice, most hunters opt for one of the commercial calls.

Using such technology to call an animal to its death appalls those who oppose hunting. They argue that these techniques are unfair and demonstrate human cruelty to animals. Hunters, on the other hand, maintain that all animals have predators and that human predators are just one type. In *A Hunter's Heart*, David Petersen wrote that, "humans evolved as predators, and nature needs predation."[19]

Many hunters maintain that humans need every advantage they can get when they stalk an animal on its native territory. Skilled duck hunters, for example, know to set up their blinds where there is a crosswind; since birds fly with the wind, a hunter with the wind at his back (the most comfortable condition on a cold fall day) will be in the poor shooting position of having the birds fly in behind him. Hunters believe that using this knowledge is just as fair as birds' hiding in marsh plants that most closely match their feathers in order to make themselves more difficult to see.

Hunting equipment specialists, however, have taken such knowledge and applied it to newer and better equipment in ways that seem to many people to have tipped the balance unfairly toward humans. Duck blinds, for example, were once permanent structures made of natural materials and had to be constructed months in advance after the hunter scouted out the best ponds. If the blind was built in one marsh and the ducks landed elsewhere, the hunter was out of luck. Today hunters can carry lightweight, portable blinds that are made of materials painted in camouflage.

Camouflage itself is controversial. Designed for armies to hide themselves from their enemies, this special clothing has been adopted by some hunters, even though many states have "blaze orange" regulations requiring big-game hunters to wear a certain percentage of bright orange on their clothing to mark them clearly and to provide protection from other hunters. Men in camouflage can look daunting and often conjure up images of Vietnam and Desert Storm in the eyes of many Americans. The *Time* magazine cover photograph of one of the boys accused in the Jonesboro schoolyard murders showed him as a toddler dressed in camouflage. The image in the mind of the reader was one of a youngster learning to kill.

Yet camouflage clothing is a multimillion-dollar business, from everyday sales at Walmart and K-mart to purchases from specialized hunting stores. Manufacturers have taken the time to create different camouflage for different occasions. For example, a pattern called Shadow Leaf issued "specially for turkey hunters and early season bow hunters."[20] Other specialized colors include Realtree X-tra Brown, Realtree X-tra Gray, and Mossy Brown Break-up.[21] First Flight by Skyline advertises that it is particularly designed for wildfowl hunting because of its "three dimensional pattern designed specifically for disguise among standing and cut corn, flooded timber, marshes and wheat stubble."[22] One of the leading manufacturers of camouflage clothing has as its slogan "It's not a passion. It's an obsession."[23] To opponents of hunting, this advertising reinforces their belief that hunters are out of control.

3

The Legacy of Hunting versus Animal Rights Activism

Any being that has the ability to experience pain or suffering has the right not to have pain and suffering inflicted upon it.

—Buzz Kemper,
Alliance for Animals

The holder of rights must have the capacity to comprehend rules of duty, governing all including themselves. Animals do not have such moral capacities.

—Carl Cohen,
"The Case Against Animal Rights"

"Bye, baby-bunting, Father's gone a-hunting, / Brother's gone to buy a skin to wrap the baby-bunting in." Generations of American mothers crooned babies to

39

sleep by singing this lullaby. Today, chances are that Daddy—and Mommy, too—have gone to work to earn money to buy blankets made of synthetic fabric in which to wrap the baby. Still the song reflects the important role that hunting has played in American culture. The frontier experience is an important part of American's heritage. Americans celebrate the time in their history when fathers hunted to provide food and clothing for their families. The frontiersman with his rifle, who beat back the wilderness and subdued wild animals has been a powerful image in our popular imagination.

Colonial American Hunters

For colonial Americans, the abundance of wild animals was just one of the many wonders of the New World. At home in England and throughout much of northern Europe, the development of agriculture had gradually destroyed the wilderness. Hunting any prey larger than rabbits, squirrels, or troublesome pests like rats was a privilege of the wealthy. The wealthy owned estates that were so large that they could set aside acres of land as private hunting preserves. Robin Hood ran afoul of the Sheriff of Nottingham by hunting on private property owned by wealthy nobles in order to get meat for his men and other poorer people.

In colonial America, the ability to hunt without restriction and without regard for one's status in society reflected the overall freedom of the new nation. Democracy in the colonies gradually took on

In colonial America, fathers and sons hunted to provide food and clothing for their families. The meat of one bear could allow a family to survive the cold winter.

many freedoms, including those of speech, religion, and the press. The freedom to hunt was a bonus. Believing that the game supply was inexhaustible in America, the early colonists put no restrictions on hunting. As Captain John Smith wrote in a pamphlet urging more Englishmen to join his Virginia colony,

> Here nature and liberty afford us that freely which in England we want, or it cost us dearly. . . . For hunting . . . the woods, lakes, and rivers afford not only chase sufficient for any that delight in that kind of toil or pleasure, but such beast to hunt that besides the delicacy of their bodies for food, their skins are so rich.[1]

The movement westward from the Atlantic Coast to settle the rest of the continent became the major pattern of human migration after 1700. Conquering new frontiers from the Appalachians to the Rocky Mountains played an important role in the settling of the United States. In fact, some historians, most famously Frederick Jackson Turner, have argued that the settling of the frontier—involving continual encounters with wild animals, dense forests, and primitive peoples—is the most important theme in American history.

Theodore Roosevelt chronicled the westward expansion and its heroes. He wrote,

> At the time when we first became a nation, nine tenths of the territory now included within the limits of the United States was wilderness. It was during the stirring and troubled years immediately preceding the outbreak of the Revolution that the most adventurous hunters, the vanguard of the hardy army of pioneer settlers, first . . . roamed through the lonely, danger-haunted forests. . . . They . . . wrought huge havoc among the herds of game with which the forests teemed. . . . While the first continental Congress was still sitting, Daniel Boone, the archetype of the American hunter, was leading his bands of tall backwoods riflemen to settle in the beautiful country of Kentucky."[2]

Roosevelt referred to Davy Crockett as "perhaps the best shot in all our country."[3] Crockett, along with Daniel Boone, who led Easterners through the mountains to the Midwest, stand as American legends, great hunters who helped create a modern country from a wilderness. Roosevelt described them as "clad in their fringed and tasselled hunting shirts of buckskin, with coonskin caps and deer-hide

Although Theodore Roosevelt was an avid hunter, he also believed that everyone should have access to the joys of the great outdoors and recognized the need to save the beauty of our vast wilderness through conservation.

leggings and moccasins."[4] Most schoolchildren know the legend that the coonskin-capped Davy Crockett "killed him a bear when he was only three." This feat marked him as the future "King of the Wild Frontier." It was no accident that Roosevelt called his first hunting/conservation club the Boone and Crockett Club.

The trappers and the farmers who moved west were hunters, as were the American Indians who had lived there long before. In eighteenth- and nineteenth-century America, hunting was not a luxury but a means of survival in frontier areas far removed

Davy Crockett was a famous frontiersman, congressman, and defender of the Alamo.

from eastern cities. Wild game was just one of the natural resources that the settlers found in abundance, along with forests and water and land.

From Frontier to Farm

Traditionally, people have marked the beginning of civilization as the time when any group stops hunting and gathering and moving from place to place, and settles down to begin farming. Traditional hunters used rocks, clubs, spears, snares, pitfalls, bow and arrow, and knives to capture animals. Tracking and stalking prey were highly developed skills.[5] When the European settlers in North America moved west, they introduced firearms to the American Indians and changed their ways of hunting forever. As the West became settled, hunting was still an honored tradition that kept the spirit of the early frontier alive.

Hunting, Religion, and Culture

The United States was a predominantly Christian nation in colonial times. Religious teachings in the

Old Testament of the Bible do not proscribe either meat-eating or hunting. In *Genesis*, the first book of the Bible, hunters and hunting are mentioned frequently, and the killing of animals for celebratory meals is common in Bible stories.

Nor does the New Testament speak out against hunting. Although there is no indication that Jesus Christ was a hunter, he most certainly fished, approved of fishing, and surrounded himself with fishermen. The Koran also does not speak for or against hunting. Whereas various dietary practices are defined for Jews and Muslims, there is nothing in their religious teachings that proscribes the killing of animals. For Americans of many traditions, then, hunting clearly has had the full stamp of religious approval and cultural acceptance in addition to both a romantic and a practical history.

From Hero Worship to Harassment

Hunting is very much a part of our American heritage. Presidents from George Washington and Abraham Lincoln to Jimmy Carter, George Bush, and Bill Clinton have enjoyed hunting for sport and relaxation. In spite of this tradition, hunting has come under increasing attack in recent years.

In Montana, just as a hunter was focusing the scope of his .308 rifle on a bison, a protester leaped between them. The hunter managed to shoot the bison, and the protester then smeared the bison's blood on the hunter's face. In Virginia, protesters blew airhorns and car horns near a wildlife refuge to

Fishing is closely akin to hunting but is not as controversial except among the most radical animal rights groups. Because fishing rarely injures human beings, it is viewed as a more benign way of obtaining food.

spook the geese before a group of licensed hunters could shoot them. In Michigan, demonstrators tied human dummies on the tops of cars and the drivers donned antlers to illustrate the reverse of what happens during deer season each fall when hunters proudly strap dead deer onto the roofs of their vehicles.

Because of these types of harassment, hunter Thomas McIntyre concluded, "At no other point in history has the idea of the hunt and the hunter been under such intense assault. . . ."[6] The assault on hunting has become so intense that in 1993 Congress passed a federal hunter harassment law. The Recreational Hunting and Safety Act makes it a federal crime to create "a hunt disruption in national forests, on public lands, in national parks, [or] on federal wild life refuges."

What has changed in American culture to shift the view of hunters as heroes to hunters as villains? Although there are many factors in modern life that contribute to antihunting sentiment, one of the greatest factors is the animal rights movement.

The Animal Rights Movement

For the past twenty-five years, the animal rights movement has been growing and gaining supporters. Although the overall number of hunters has also grown, the percentage of people who hunt in the United States has been declining. More Americans live in urban areas. They do not hunt, and they do not have close friends who hunt. This statement is important, because polls indicate that people's feelings about hunting are directly affected by whether or not they know any hunters personally. Those who do know hunters personally are far more likely to tolerate, and be less likely to oppose, hunting.

There are many different types of animal rights organizations. Most of the major conservation groups do not oppose hunting. They believe that hunting is a useful tool in wildlife management. The question of animal rights is a separate one from that of conservation. Some moderate animal rights advocates do not oppose all hunting, but instead concentrate on insuring that there is legislation for the humane means of killing animals. Other groups oppose all forms of hunting but limit themselves to nonviolent protest. A very small minority of animal rights activists not only oppose all hunting, but believe that it is necessary to take violent actions to stop hunters.[7]

Most hunters are worried about the impact that animal rights groups are having on hunting. One of them summarized the conflict:

> The animal rights movement is getting so much support because it is also tapping into our concerns about safety, personal freedom, ecological balance, racial equality, power and powerlessness, violence, terrorism, and the tendency of the media to sensationalize news to compete for ratings.[8]

Do Animals Have Rights?

The basic question to this issue is the following: Do animals have rights? Borrowing some of their ideas

Using a real animal carcass for target practice is the kind of thing that particularly outrages animal rights activists.

from the late twentieth-century civil rights and women's movements, antihunting advocates argue that when humans kill animals for food, they are trampling on the rights of animals, a minority group.

On the other side of the question, people who favor hunting believe that animals have no rights because they cannot make moral judgments. Asked author Carl Cohen, "Does a lion have a right to eat a baby zebra? Does a baby zebra have a right not to be eaten?"[9] Cohen maintained that speciesism—viewing one species, humans, as superior to all others—is not the same as sexism or racism. He maintained that carrying laws against speciesism to their natural conclusion would be impossible and absurd. He wrote, "At great human cost, the lives of fish and crustaceans must also be protected with equal vigor if speciesism has been forsworn."[10]

Most hunters argue that animals, by the working of nature, end up as prey. They also argue that animals do not have rights in the same way that people have rights. Ethical hunters, however, do not believe in the wanton killing of any animal.

Hunting, Animal Rights, and Death

Animal rights activists think that the killing of animals is the ultimate crime of the hunter. They view the death of any animal for human use as unnecessary and cruel. Hunting advocates point out that the average animal rights activist is a woman in her forties who has a college education and an average income of $40,000, lives in an urban area, and owns several pets. Many hunters believe that urban dwellers are not qualified to make a judgment about the cruelty of hunting.

Hunters argue that humans are simply one type of predator—and the most successful—in the animal kingdom. José Ortega y Gasset, a Spanish philosopher-statesman, wrote an analysis of the philosophy of hunting. He noted, "There is hardly a class or phylum in which groups of hunting animals do not appear. The cat hunts rats. The lion hunts antelope. The sphex and other wasps hunt caterpillars and grubs. The shark hunts smaller fish. The bird of prey hunts rabbits and doves."[11]

Another hunter described his first successful shot with a BB gun when he was a young boy: "The BB went exactly where I had aimed and the bird crumpled. I was awestruck. . . . In that moment I realized that I had the power of life and death in my hands when I had a gun."[12]

Dragging a deer through the woods after it has been killed is hard work. Traditional hunters carry out their meat on foot and dress the animal themselves.

President Jimmy Carter wrote of the relationship between death and food this way:

> I was brought up in an agricultural society where chickens, hogs, sheep, goats and cattle were raised for food. There was no real distinction in my mind between those animals and the quail, doves, ducks, squirrels and rabbits that also arrived on our table after a successful hunt.[13]

Animal rights advocates argue that the society of Carter's childhood no longer needs to exist in modern America. Hunters accuse animal rights advocates of selecting the parts of the past they want to honor. They claim that animal rights advocates often invoke American Indian culture in their arguments about humans' relationship with the animal world, but ignore hunting as an integral part of American Indian life. Hunters cite American Indians such as the Navajo medicine man—and hunter—Claus Chee Sonny, who said that "our life, our breath, and our thoughts are given to us by the plants and animals we eat," but that life in urban and suburban America has created the illusion that "we can have food without harvest, that life can be maintained without death."[14]

Animal Rights and Hunting Ethics

Cleveland Amory, one of this country's most avid animal rights activists, founded the Fund for Animals. The Fund is one of the best-organized, most vocal, and most successful animal rights organizations in the country today. Its members oppose all hunting and work actively to stop it. They agree with

Amory's statement that "Hunting is an antiquated expression of macho self-aggrandizement, with no place in civilized society."[15]

Whereas many Americans do not agree with the Fund for Animals and other animal rights activists who advocate the total abolition of hunting, they do have negative feelings about hunters. And it is the behavior of that group of hunters dubbed "slob hunters" that gives the animal rights activists their best ammunition in the fight against hunting.

Trophy Hunters

Many hunters and nonhunters alike reserve their greatest scorn for trophy hunters. These are people who hunt, not for the meat or the experience of being outdoors, but rather for the pleasure and bragging rights of killing the biggest or rarest animal possible. These hunters tend to be wealthy and are willing to pay a great deal of money for guides to take them to remote places all over the world where the trophy animals might live. If the hunt is successful, these hunters display the stuffed heads or antlers of their kill as trophies on their walls and get their name in the record books.

Trophy hunters make up a minority of all hunters. They justify their hunting by arguing that the largest animals are the oldest animals and the most likely to die. By killing them as trophies and then preserving them as mounts on walls, they insure that the animal will be immortalized. Although our greatest hunter/conservationist president, Theodore

Roosevelt, was a trophy hunter, the days of trophy hunting are numbered. As the hunter Thomas McIntyre put it, "What [trophy hunting] has to do with hunting . . . is utterly beyond me. . . . When a man begins to see game strictly in terms of inches on a steel tape or a ranking on the page of a record book . . . the game, the *true* game is over."[16]

The Battle for Young People's Opinions

To preserve hunting against the charges of animal cruelty and barbaric behavior that the animal rights activists have leveled against them, hunters could support laws against unethical practices such as baiting animals with unusual foods and hounding them by chasing them with dogs; oppose hunting purely for trophies; turn in poachers who violate the rules of fair chase; refuse to participate in contest hunting; respect other people's property by not littering and by getting permission in advance to hunt on private land; avoid displaying dead animals; and limit the uses of modern technology.

Adults who hunt, especially men, are most likely to have hunted when they were young, so animal rights activists are trying to convert young people to their cause by bringing their literature and programs into schools. Most students today, like most adults, live in urban areas and do not know many, if any, hunters personally. Cartoons such as *Bambi*, *Fern Gully,* and *Seabert the Seal* give animals human personalities and reinforce the idea that hunters hurt animals. In *Bambi*, for example, the fawn loses his mother when she is killed by a hunter, and in *Seabert* the message is clearly articulated that "wild animals are disappearing from earth because man is hunting them."[17] Hunters point out that the view of nature in both *Bambi* and *Fern Gully* is terribly unrealistic. Humans are not the only enemy the animals have, and all the animals do not get along with one anther. Thumper the rabbit and Owl, both friends of Bambi, are also friends of each other—but in reality, owls are the deadly enemy of rabbits.

Most animal rights groups have special programs that target students in school. The Humane Society of the United States, the American Anti-Vivisection Society and PETA (People for the Ethical Treatment of Animals) have junior branches. They distribute booklets and fact sheets and instruct children about ways that they can help in the campaign for animal rights. Their Web sites have special junior links.

The tactics they encourage vary. Some are non-controversial to hunters and nonhunters alike; students are urged to learn more about animals and their habitats, to support conservation, and to treat pets humanely. The Humane Society of the United States, however, publishes a pamphlet that explains how to organize an animal rights group in a school. Its list of activities includes boycotting rodeos, circuses, and zoos where, it claims, animals are mistreated for the pleasure of humans.

Other tactics are more controversial. For example, in a PETA booklet, "Kids Can Save the Animals," readers are urged to tie up the telephone lines of businesses that do research using animals. PETA supporters have also urged teenagers to picket pet shops and stores selling fur coats. The Humane Society of the United States urges junior members to practice hunter harassment. Hunters are invariably portrayed in a negative light. A recent PETA Web site commentary, capitalizing on the habits of slob hunters, noted that where there are hunters and fishermen, "there's usually a trail of trash."[18] Animal rights groups believe that they are making converts among their younger supporters. A Gallup poll in 1991 indicated that 41 percent of American teenagers support animal rights "very much." Whether this means that they will support legislation to outlaw hunting remains to be seen. So far, animal rights activists have helped outlaw air hunting in Alaska, commercial trapping of wolves, bearbaiting in California, elk hunting in the Cocomino National Forest in Arizona, grizzly hunting in Montana, and the hounding and baiting of bears in Colorado and Oregon.

4

Hunting and Conservation

*[Hunting] fosters a caring attitude toward
the environment, which leads to environ-
mentally sensitive behavior.*
> —*The Council for Wildlife
Conservation and Education*

*[Between the ages of 12 and 18] I reveled in
killing, maiming, bloodletting and gutting.
Never did I have the slightest thoughts
regarding carrying capacity, overbrowsing,
population dynamics or any other game
management concept.*
> —*Steve Rugger, "Why I Don't Hunt"*

Like the animal rights movement, the
conservation movement is inextricably tied
to hunting. Prominent hunters such as
Theodore Roosevelt, Henry Cabot Lodge,

and George Bird Grinnell were pioneers in the American conservation movement at the end of the nineteenth century. At the same time, magazines such as *Sports Afield* and *Outdoor Life*, which are filled with hunting stories and advice, began as journals intended to educate people about the need for conserving wild animal resources. Hunters maintain that they are more aware of and concerned about the environment and about the preservation of animal habitat than other people are, because without animals there could be no hunting. Opponents of hunting claim that hunters focus too narrowly on preserving the habitat and on increasing the numbers of only their favorite prey, for example—elk, wildfowl, white-tailed deer, and wild turkeys.

The Link Between Hunters and Conservation

Although much of the argument on both sides of the question is emotional, some indisputable facts link hunting and the conservation movement. First, planned conservation in the United States is a twentieth-century phenomenon that got its start when a group of dedicated hunters, led by Theodore Roosevelt, became concerned about the possible extinction of a number of animals that had once been plentiful in this country. Second, most members of present-day conservation groups and conservation officers do not oppose hunting. In fact, they are likely to be hunters themselves, and they often view hunting as a valuable tool in the overall conservation and management of wild animals. Third, hunting and fishing licensing fees, along with special taxes on hunting and fishing equipment, are the major source of funding for state wildlife management programs.

In 1969, Congress recognized the role that generations of hunters and fishermen have played in conservation by declaring a day to be set aside each fall as National Hunting and Fishing Day. In establishing this day, Congress was continuing a nearly century-old national tradition: federal support for both hunting and conservation.

Opponents of hunting are correct in recognizing humans as animals' fiercest predators. Wherever human beings have interacted with wild animals, the animals have lost. Anthropologists speculate that before humans crossed the Bering Strait to North America, cheetahs, elephants, lions, and beavers as big as bears roamed the continent. In the Pacific Islands thousands of years ago, the arrival of Polynesian people resulted in the destruction of thousands of bird species. Since the arrival of Captain James Cook in the Hawaiian Islands at the end of the eighteenth century, one third of Hawaii's bird species have become extinct.

Habitat Conservation

Although human interaction with wild game has often resulted in the destruction of animal species, it is not clear that hunting alone is responsible for this destruction. Hunters, and many conservationists, argue that it is not hunting but the destruction of animal habitats that causes the death of so many animals and, therefore, the extinction of some species. When land was cleared for farming in colonial New England, when acres of the West were fenced in for ranching, many animal habitats were destroyed. Similarly, today when marshlands are drained for a shopping mall, animal habitats are destroyed.

Hunters are vitally concerned about the destruction of animals' habitats. A great portion of their conservation efforts is directed at the preservation of these habitats so that wild animals can continue to thrive in an increasingly urban nation. Hunters support programs to protect land from development.

A major component of wildlife management programs is the conservation of forest areas and wetlands where wild animals can live. As one conservationist observed, "Cover [forests, high grass, bushes, etc.] . . . represents the animals' combined maternity ward, nursery, bedroom, dining room, living room, tornado shelter and bomb shelter."[1] A major use of money from hunters' fees is buying land to create public wildlife refuges. Opponents of hunting believe that all hunting should be banned on such refuges. Hunters believe that hunting helps maintain stable animal populations in these areas.

When the first European settlers landed in the colonies, wildfowl thrived on millions of acres of wetland. Today, over half of those wetlands have been drained for human purposes. In California, Illinois, and Connecticut, 90 percent of each state's wetlands has been destroyed. Between 1954 and 1994, the duck population of Indiana declined from one million

Some animal habitats are under constant threat of becoming land development projects such as shopping malls and roads. Wildlife management and conservation groups help prevent this development from happening.

to nine thousand. During that same period of time, Indiana lost 87 percent of its wetlands to developers. Wetlands are vital to ducks' survival. As one hunter and conservationist note, "Bogs, swamps, and marshes are being gobbled up by farms, roads, parking lots, subdivisions, and malls at the alarming rate of 650 acres a day—over 300,000 acres a year."[2]

Hunting today does not threaten the extinction of any legally hunted animal species. But between the time of European settlement and the end of the nineteenth century, hunting was a leading cause of the reduction of animal resources in the United States. Responsible hunters, however, launched the conservation movement to stop this destruction.

From Land of Plenty to Land of Scarcity

When the early colonists landed in the New World, they found a land teeming with wild game. They needed skill with firearms, along with hunting and trapping techniques learned from American Indians, to provide food, clothing, and shelter.

In addition, from the nation's earliest beginnings, it was clear that there was a profit to be made in selling the meat and skins of wild animals. French trappers pushed into the Mississippi River Valley in pursuit of furs that could be sold in Europe. Hunting and trapping in the seventeenth and eighteenth centuries, however, led to the near extinction of the American beaver, pine marten, and fisher. The Americans who followed the French trapping tradition in the nineteenth century continued the destruction. The beaver, a very adaptable animal, even changed its habits to elude its human predators. Over time the beaver became a nocturnal animal that worked in the dark and slept by day to better escape the hunter.

Market Hunting

Market hunting, the killing of wild animals for commercial sale, reached its peak in the first century after the American Revolution. Market hunting nearly destroyed game animals in the United States. Market hunters were often seen as romantic figures who told tales about the wild animals they encountered. Their hunting, so easy to condemn in retrospect, was not illegal at this time.

In the early twentieth century, market hunters, such as this one photographed in the 1920s, regaled their listeners with tales of a time when game was plentiful.

Market hunters exploited wildlife during a period when many of America's rich natural resources were being widely misused. There were no restrictions on the number of animals or birds a market hunter could take. In the late nineteenth century,

> wildlife was given little value except as a commercial resource. The variety of wild animals that could be sold profitably for their meat, feathers, or fur was the raw material of the market hunters' enterprise. And in an age when restrictions and controls on business were practically unknown, the commercial gunner maximized his profits by taking all he could as often as he could.[3]

In the nineteenth century, lumber camps and grand tourist hotels alike listed venison and other game on their menus, and deer and other animals were hunted legally year-round. All hunting methods were legal. Hounding—chasing a deer with dogs, is illegal today, but it was a common practice then and was immortalized in many famous paintings. Jacklighting deer at night—or freezing them in the glow of a lantern so they would be clear targets— another practice outlawed today, was also common.

For market hunters, quantity was the key to making a profit, so the more animals they could take, the better. A dozen fisher pelts, sold in the city, might equal a year's wages for a farmer. In 1871, the bounty on a wolf was $30 and on a panther, $20. This was at a time when a good wage in a factory was $1.50 for a ten-hour day.[4]

On August 1, 1914, an old passenger pigeon

named Martha died at the Cincinnati Zoo. With her death, the passenger pigeon became extinct. Passenger pigeons, which had once been so numerous that flocks of them numbered in the millions and could obscure the sun like a dark cloud, no longer existed. Like the American bison, the Michigan wolverine, the California grizzly bear, and the Carolina parakeet, the passenger pigeon was the victim of market hunting. The pigeon, in fact, was the most common item on restaurant menus in the late nineteenth century. Its popularity hastened its extinction at the hands of market hunters.

Buffalo, a type of bison, once roamed the western United States in herds of thousands. Nineteenth-century hunters nearly eliminated the buffalo from the country.

The Beginning of Conservation

By the last quarter of the nineteenth century, the wood duck was almost extinct, the white-tailed deer population had shrunk dramatically, the passenger pigeon was well on its way to obliteration, and only a few bison remained. If wild animals were to remain in the United States, steps would have to be taken to conserve them. The first group to recognize this need for conservation were hunters, who noticed that their game was becoming scarcer and scarcer.

Theodore Roosevelt's Boone and Crockett Club was followed in 1892 by the Sierra Club and in 1905 by the Audubon Society. These organizations remain in existence today and are considered models for conservation and environmental protection. None of those groups oppose hunting in principle. Boone and Crockett actively promotes hunting, including the idea of "fair chase," and other principles of good sportsmanship. Boone and Crockett also maintains detailed records of trophy animals taken in North America.

Hunters, Conservation, and the Law

These conservation groups believe that one of the best ways to conserve the nation's animal resources is by using the power of the government. They also support legislation that regulated hunting and fishing practices. They also have sponsored the idea of state licensing fees to pay the salaries of professional wildlife managers and game wardens. They work to

By designating campsites or building private lodges for hunters, wildlife management groups can keep track of the many hunters who are permitted to use the land during the season.

have the government set aside land as wildlife refuges.

In 1872, Yellowstone National Park was established as a national wildlife and land preserve. In 1886, New York State included in its constitution one of the farthest-reaching plans for wildlife refuge developed by any state before or since. Thousands of acres of land in the Adirondacks were preserved as "forever wild."

In 1891, Yellowstone Park and the Adirondack preserve paved the way for a federal law authorizing the president to withdraw lands from the public domain and give them to the Department of the Interior to manage as national parks and refuges.

When he became president in 1901, Theodore Roosevelt used this law to set aside fifty federal animal refuges. He helped create five new national parks and established the federal Forest Service. Roosevelt is considered by most historians to be the father of modern conservation.

Protecting Animals

Beginning in 1895 and for the next twenty-five years, New York passed an aggressive series of laws designed to reverse the damage to animal resources. The state created a white-tailed deer season limited from mid-August to late October, outlawed night hunting, and prohibited the sale of venison. Similar laws protected other animals. Soon other states followed New York's lead in protecting their wildlife.

In the early decades of the twentieth century, game populations increased. Hunting advocates point to the initiation of this legislation as evidence of the positive role that hunters have played in conservation. Since the 1920s, the white-tailed deer population of the United States has jumped from 30,000 to 20 million, wild turkey from 30,000 to 4 million, pronghorn antelope from 25,000 to 1 million, and elk from 50,000 to 1 million. Wood ducks, which were nearly extinct, are now the most common waterfowl in the eastern United States.

Opponents of hunting note, however, that the gains in animal population have come mostly in game animals. They argue that hunters, even national heroes such as Roosevelt, have been interested in

When this deer was killed in the Adirondacks in the 1920s, the white-tailed deer population of New York was just beginning to rebound after years of hunting without regulation.

preserving animals only in order to shoot them. They believe that a hunter's real interest in conservation is limited by self-interest.

Licensing and Conservation

A major part of the wildlife legislation in the late nineteenth century was the licensing of hunters and fishermen. In 1908, New York was the first state to require a hunting license. Within twenty years, every state had followed New York's example. The license fees were used to pay for the programs and personnel to manage the new laws regulating hunting. As a result of this program, game wardens and wildlife management officials were dependent on hunting and fishing for their salaries.

Opponents of hunting disapprove of this connection. They have a number of complaints. First, too many of the people who are hired to manage wildlife, and whose salaries depend on hunters' fees, favor hunting and put the needs of hunters over the needs of animals. Second, wildlife managers do not consider alternatives to hunting in their wildlife management programs. Finally, wildlife managers are under great pressure from hunting organizations to preserve game animals and do not spend as much time preserving animals that are of little value to hunters.

Whether or not the fears of those opposing hunting are legitimate, it is true that hunting and fishing licenses are extremely important sources of funds for wildlife management programs. Over the years since the 1920s, hunting licenses and permits have raised $8 billion, which has been used by state wildlife management programs. The money has been used to acquire new habitat, to improve refuges that the states already owned, to pay for law enforcement, and to implement hunter education programs for adults and young people. In 1996 an estimated 15 million licensed hunters contributed over $500 million to the budgets of state fish and wildlife agencies. When fishing license fees are added to the figure, it nearly doubles.

In addition to state fees, the federal government also collects hunting and fishing fees. In 1934, the Federal Duck Stamp Act was passed, requiring all hunters of waterfowl to purchase a special stamp to place on their hunting licenses. Revenue from these stamps reached over $20 million a year in the late 1990s and was used to purchase over 5 million acres of wetlands to be used as wildfowl refuges.

Three years after the passage of the Duck Stamp Act, Congress passed the Federal Aid in Wildlife Restoration Act (also known as the Pittman-Robertson Act). In order to procure even more funds for federal programs to protect wildlife, the law placed special excise taxes on archery and fishing equipment, guns, and ammunition. In other words, taxes were put on the equipment that hunters and fishermen purchased. The money raised from these taxes was $165.8 million in 1997 alone and has totaled $3.2 billion overall since they were first collected. This money has been distributed to the states for their fish and wildlife management programs.

Hunters and Habitat Preservation

Hunters call themselves "America's First Environmentalists" and claim that "Virtually every species of wildlife, from songbirds and chipmunks to bald eagles and whooping cranes, benefits from the programs supported and financed by hunters and anglers."[5] They point out that hunters pay nine times as much per person as the average citizen to maintain protected public lands where nonhunters can hike, camp, boat, and observe nature. Pittman-Robertson funds have been used to establish more than four thousand state wildlife management areas totaling 45 million acres of land. Although these are important sites for hunters, 75 percent of the people who use these areas do not hunt. Opponents of hunting believe that these areas should be financed in a different way and that hunting should be prohibited on all public land.

Hunters and nonhunters alike agree on the importance of conserving the natural habitat for wild animals. Hunters believe that the destruction of habitat is the most dangerous threat facing game animals today. This destruction threatens the future of hunting as well. Although hunters do not dispute the destruction that past practices such as market hunting had on wildlife species, they nevertheless believe that some species died and others have survived because of their ability or inability to adapt to changing habitat conditions. Hunters believe that the elimination of wild habitat by growing farms and towns is just as destructive as market hunting.

There are more subtle conservation issues. Many who disapprove of hunting are vegetarians. They do not believe in killing any animal for food. Most of the grains produced in the United States today are produced on enormous farms. In fact, farming today is often referred to as *agribusiness*, a term that reflects its size and profit motive. In the recent past, these farms were wetlands, forest, and other natural habitats for animals. Planting and harvesting grains on a large scale destroys the habitats of songbirds, reptiles, and small mammals. One Oregon farmer admitted that,

> half the cottontail rabbits went into his combine when he cut a wheat field, that virtually all of the small mammals, ground birds, and reptiles were killed when he harvested windrow crops like rye and sugar beets, and that when the leaves were stripped from the bush beans all the mice and snakes who were living among them were destroyed as well.[6]

Conservationists are also concerned about how humans use all of the earth's natural resources, not just wild animals. The energy needed to produce grains and beans can equal or surpass the energy needed to produce wild game. An elk hunter who shoots an elk near his home in the Rocky Mountains can provide his family with 150 pounds of meat. Counting his clothing, ammunition, transportation to the hunting area, and the energy needed to store the meat in the freezer, the cost of procuring this food is about 80,000 kilocalories. Providing the same family with enough beans and rice to replace the food value of the meat would cost 500,000 kilocalories. Energy costs of processes such as irrigation, transportation costs, and the cost of farm equipment and packaging are taken into account. In terms of damage to the total resources of the earth, hunters argue that killing meat is less costly than the intensive vegetable, fruit, and grain growth that would be required to maintain a modern American vegetarian diet. As the elk hunter in the aforementioned example concluded, "Is the elk shot by me any more or less a necessary death than . . . that of the thousands of rabbits and mice inadvertently destroyed in the process of growing and harvesting my organic, all natural, oat bran breakfast cereal?"[7]

Hunting as Wildlife Management Tool

Wildlife management ensures that the number and variety of game animals in an area remain at the best levels for the carrying capacity of the area. *Carrying capacity* is the term for a habitat's ability to provide food and safe shelter for the animals that live there. When an animal population grows larger than the area's ability to provide food for all the animals, it is said to have exceeded its carrying capacity. When that happens, hunting is one method that can be used to reduce that animal's numbers. Hunters and many wildlife managers argue that without hunting, the numbers of many game animals, most notably deer, would spiral out of control. Opponents argue that there are more effective and more humane means of animal population control.

In the 1780s, Daniel Boone wrote to John James Audubon about the plentiful deer around his settlement in Kentucky. In amazement he commented, "You would not have walked out in any direction for more than a mile without shooting a buck."[8]

A good illustration of how the deer population has decreased and increased can be found in Iowa County, Wisconsin. In this county, where deer were once plentiful, all deer hunting was prohibited from

Most states prohibit hunting ducks in the spring because that is when the females care for their young.

1907 to 1942 because the deer had nearly disappeared. By the 1950s, hunters were taking 50 to 60 deer per season, and in recent years, the number has topped 10,000 deer. By 1900, market hunting for venison and skins had reduced the white-tailed deer population to a few thousand. Between 1900 and today, the deer population has grown astronomically.

Deer are the most popular target of hunters. Hunters kill four times as many white-tailed deer annually as could be found in the entire country in 1900.

The growth in the deer population has coincided with a growing animosity toward hunting and the growth in absolute numbers of deer hunters. Although hunters stalk many kinds of animals, in the public's mind, deer are the animals most often associated with hunting. A deer carcass strapped to the roof of a car is the autumn image that is most repellent to those who disapprove of hunting. The average life expectancy for a white-tailed deer in the wild is more than eight years. In heavily hunted areas, the life expectancy drops to two years. How then, can hunting have contributed to the growth of the deer population? The answer lies in wildlife management—the regulations that limit how and when deer can be taken.

Deer Management

Wildlife management depends heavily on the work of biologists who study animals' life cycles and breeding habits, monitor their diseases, and keep track of the type, location, and quantity of their natural predators. Deer hunting seasons occur in the fall and often coincide with the time in the deer's natural cycle known as the rut. During rut, bucks (male deer) seek out does (female deer) with whom to mate. This period ensures that there will be fawns in the spring. Deer hunters learn the habits of the male deer in order to track them. They know, for example, that a white-tailed buck will rub his horns against a tree and leave his scent on the ground in an area he has pawed (this is called a scrape). These habits, meant

The white-tailed deer is the most common prey for hunters in the United States today.

to attract does, also attract the keen eye of the skilled hunter.

The first hunting regulations limited most hunters to taking bucks. However, since the 1950s, with the growing presence of deer in suburban areas, wildlife managers have encouraged the taking of does as well as bucks. Hunting is an important deer management tool in agricultural areas where maintaining a stable deer population is critical to the success of crops. Deer are notorious for feeding on crops and gardens. As one deer specialist put it, "Deer will eat just about anything you can plant."[9]

The deer population potentially doubles every two years because the average doe has fifteen fawns during a lifetime of eight years. Biologists measure the number of deer an area can feed and suggest bag limits and doe seasons to control the population. To maintain a stable deer population at the current number of 16 million deer nationwide, fully 40 percent of all deer could be taken each season. Instead, hunters take about 25 percent, so the deer population continues to grow.

Opponents of hunting are aware of this growth, but they feel that methods other than hunting should be used to limit it. Among the ways they propose are sterilization, trapping deer in live traps and then transplanting them, and introducing natural predators to an area. Hunters contend that sterilizing an animal, which is not always practical because the animal must be caught first, demonstrates a greater degree of human disruption of the environment than hunting does. Female elk, for example, choose the bucks with the largest antlers to father their babies because large antlers indicate a healthy animal. If the largest bucks were sterilized, the elk population in an area could conceivably weaken.

Live traps and transplanting require that the government add more land to wildlife refuges in order for there to be some place for the trapped animals to be released. In addition, transplanting often injures the wild animals who may become terrified or disoriented when they are captured. Natural predators of deer, such as the timber wolf, are now being reintroduced to the Adirondacks. The timber wolf has the potential to keep the deer population naturally under control, but the possibility exists that the wolf population may grow out of control and exceed the carrying capacity of the region. Such predators also pose a threat to domestic animals.

Perhaps the biggest obstacle facing these other methods of wildlife management is expense. Hunting and fishing fees provide three quarters of the revenue for wildlife management programs. If hunting is no longer allowed, this source of income will diminish severely at the same time that more expensive management techniques are put into effect. Tax money will have to be raised to pay for the new programs.

The situation at the National Elk Refuge in Wyoming illustrates some of the problems of wildlife management. In 1912, nearly 25,000 acres of land was set aside by the federal government as a refuge for elk. By the 1990s, the herd, fed and protected by park rangers, had grown too big for the area and needed to be culled. The decision was made to issue a limited number of special hunting licenses and to allow some elk to be killed. Although there was a great deal of outcry from nonhunters about this decision, other solutions to limiting the herd seemed not to be preferable. Cutting feed in the winter would have meant death by starvation. Reintroducing wolves would have brought about other risks. State officials wanted to use the prime real estate that borders the refuge for homes and ranching, not for elk grazing. Sterilization is expensive and upsets the natural selection process.

As the residential and agricultural development of the United States claims more wildlife habitat,

Sometimes reintroducing a natural predator, such as the wolf, helps manage the balance of numbers in deer and elk herds.

issues of wildlife management—and the role that hunting should play in that management—will be ever more critical. Providing space for the wild animals that have lived in North America for thousands of years is a conservation issue that will need thoughtful decisions from nonhunters and hunters alike.

Endangered Species

It is clear that market hunting helped lead to the extinction of some animals. Hunters claim that since the end of market hunting, human beings have not been directly responsible for the extinction of any species by hunting. Yet awareness of endangered species and their protection are major parts of the modern conservation movement.

Because endangered species cannot be legally hunted, it may be difficult at first to see the connection between endangered species and hunting. However, it is the fees from hunting and fishing that fund the U.S. Fish and Wildlife Service, the agency responsible for protecting and reviving endangered species. Hunters maintain that because of their financial support, which funds the U.S. Fish and Wildlife Service, they do more than any other single group of citizens to help protect threatened wildlife.

There are more than four hundred animals (and another 400 plants) on the endangered list in the United States. In 1995, the U.S. Fish and Wildlife Service spent $79.3 million to protect endangered species. Although hunters and nonhunters alike accept that human activities have been the greatest reason for species' extinction, there is a great deal of controversy over the role that hunting has played.

Conservation of all our natural resources, whether endangered or plentiful, is a growing concern to Americans. As long as the conservation of animals is heavily paid for by the minority of the population that hunts, conservation and hunting will be thoroughly intertwined.

5

Hunting and Gun Control

Addressing the violence in our schools, our streets and our homes requires that we reject the conventional wisdom that killing animals is an acceptable part of growing up.

—Dr. Randall Lockwood,
Humane Society of the United States

Repeatedly, I have observed the resourcefulness and stability of young men who have had an opportunity to learn how to take care of themselves as . . . hunters. . . .
—President Dwight D. Eisenhower

The United States has a reputation for being one of the most violent nations in the civilized world. That reputation is well earned. Americans kill more of their fellow

83

citizens in a day than the Japanese do in a year. There are more murders in the United States each week than there are in all of Western Europe in a year. School shootings such as the 1999 Littleton, Colorado, Columbine High School murder/suicide make worldwide headlines. Gun laws in the United States are more liberal than they are in any other modern industrialized country in the world. It is very easy for American citizens to buy and own guns that are forbidden in most other countries.

Hunters argue that there is no direct connection between hunting and the high rate of murder due to firearms. They claim that "among cultures around the world where hunting was a primary activity, people tended to be peaceful."[1] Hunting advocates maintain that there is no evidence that hunters are more likely to commit murder than nonhunters. Hunting advocates argue that Adolf Hitler and Charles Manson, two people guilty of ruthless, cold-blooded behavior, were both vegetarians. They also state that there are at least ten times more guns in the United States than there are hunters and that guns owned by the untrained general populace are far more dangerous than guns owned by responsible, well-trained hunters. In California, the state with the lowest percentage of hunters, more than 600,000 guns were sold in 1993. Nearly 450,000 of them were handguns or other weapons not appropriate for hunting game.[2]

On the other hand, opponents of hunting point to the high correlation between incidents of gun violence and areas where hunters are prevalent.

Louisiana has the highest murder rate of any state in the country. Its license plates proudly bear the state's motto—"Sportsmen's Paradise"—a tribute to its tradition of hunting and fishing.

The nation was stunned on March 9, 1998, when two young boys who were both hunters, aged eleven and thirteen, opened fire on their schoolmates in Jonesboro, Arkansas, killing four of them. Critics of hunting were quick to point out that Arkansas is the state with the greatest percentage of hunters in the general population and that a majority of the children in Arkansas grow up in households where guns are present.

Opponents contend that hunting leads to accidental deaths and that the sport is highly dangerous. Not only do animals suffer and die during hunting season, but every year hunters and innocent bystanders are maimed and killed as well. In addition, children and adults die by the hundreds every year at home, in accidents involving guns that are used for hunting.

Hunters and Safety

Many Americans are familiar with the story of Karen Wood. A Maine housewife, Wood was hanging out her wash on a cold autumn day in 1989 when a hunter mistook the white mittens she was wearing for the rump of a whitetail deer. He shot and killed the woman in her own backyard. A grand jury found the hunter innocent of any crime. A local Maine newspaper editorialized that Karen Wood was responsible for her own death because she was not wearing blaze orange when she knew it was hunting season.

Stories such as this one heighten people's anxiety about the dangers of hunting. However, hunters in most states have to pass a hunter safety course before they can receive their licenses, and those safety courses include mandatory sections on gun safety. No responsible hunters shoot at a flash of white. Instead, they are taught that their target and the area beyond the target must be clearly and completely visible before they fire. The National Rifle Association (NRA) sponsors numerous children's hunter safety clinics. In their magazine and on their Web site, they have a cartoon character named Eddie Eagle who teaches children the dos and don'ts of gun safety. The NRA maintains that the Eddie Eagle character helps children become responsible gun owners and hunters, but those who favor gun control view Eddie Eagle differently. The Violence Policy Center, for example, sees this as an "'educational' program actually designed to recruit new gun consumers rather than teach gun safety."[3]

Many hunters and nonhunters alike believe the typical ten-hour course required by most states is inadequate. They cite the hunter courses in Europe, where the hunting accident rate is extremely low. In most European countries, the hunter course is one hundred hours long. In addition to weapons safety, prospective hunters are taught first aid, conservation, and animal identification skills.

In 1990, there were 146 deaths from hunting in

The young girl in this picture, who is about to hunt with her father for the first time, is accustomed to living with guns at home.

the United States. The number has been decreasing annually during this decade. According to the National Safety Council, hunting is safer than swimming, boating, or driving a car. Many more people are killed each year by drowning, in car accidents, in fires, and even in falls around their homes than are killed in hunting accidents. Hunting has become safer during the twentieth century. In 1909, there was on the average, one hunter death per ninety deer taken; today the average is one death for every 88,000 deer taken.

In New York State the accident rate has been cut in half over the last thirty years, from fourteen deaths in 1962 to one death in 1994 and an average annual death rate in the last decade of six deaths. At the start of the 1997 whitetail season Mike O'Hara, who works for the New York Department of Environmental Conservation, commented, "A hunter making a one-hour drive is ten times more likely to be injured in a traffic accident than spending an entire day in the field."[4] O'Hara and other hunters

This picture of a hunter, his family, and two deer killed in the Adirondacks was taken in 1907, a year before the first hunting licenses were required by the state of New York.

contended that following the basic firearms safety rules that are taught in hunter education courses "can prevent virtually all hunting injuries."[5]

Statistics indicate that deaths such as Karen Wood's in Maine are rare. Most hunting deaths do not involve innocent bystanders. Instead the victims are hunters who accidentally kill themselves or members of their own hunting party. Nationally, statistics show that a person is more likely to be killed by lightning than in a hunting accident.[6] In California, for example, only one person was injured and no one was killed during a recent hunting season when a half million people were hunting.[7]

Hunters and Gun Control

Luke T. Woodham, a teenager, was found guilty of murdering several classmates at his high school in Pearl, Mississippi, in the fall of 1997. In addressing the jury at Woodham's trial, the district attorney who was prosecuting the case said, "[This] was a criminal act, a mean act, an act of murder that was committed with a rifle you hunt deer with."[8] No one, not even the murderer, disputed the lawyer's statement. However, whether or not the banning of hunting would lead to the end of murders such as the ones committed by Woodham is not completely clear.

Gun control advocates often target hunters as the source of many murder weapons, particularly those used by children to kill other children. If hunting guns were not allowed, then teenagers such as Luke Woodham, Kip Kinkel (who killed classmates in

Springfield, Oregon), and children such as Mitchell Johnson and Andrew Golden (the shooters in the Jonesboro, Arkansas, case) would not have such easy access to lethal weapons.

According to those who oppose hunting, there would be far fewer guns in people's homes if there were no hunting. Young people would not have access to guns, and firearms murders, both planned and unplanned, would be reduced. Hunters respond that accidents do not happen to responsible hunters who follow appropriate safety rules and also keep their guns under secure control.

Although accidental deaths from hunting are declining, the number of childhood deaths by firearms is on the increase. The number of children killed by firearms increased by 153 percent in the decade between 1985 and 1995. In 1995, nearly two hundred children under the age of fifteen were shot and killed. This is the highest rate of childhood death by guns in the entire world. The National Centers for Disease Control estimate that at current rates, death by gunfire will be the leading cause of product-related death among children by the year 2003.[9] People who oppose hunting claim that there is a link between these deaths and the presence of hunting guns in people's houses.

The 1999 massacre in Littleton, Colorado, at Columbine High School presents another example of young people's easy access to guns and bomb-making materials. In April 1999, two students entered the school with dozens of homemade bombs, as well as two shotguns, a TEC 9 semiautomatic pistol, and a

9mm semiautomatic rifle. Before the young gunmen committed suicide, they had killed twelve of their fellow students and one teacher, as well as injuring or shooting dozens of other students. It was the worst school massacre in history. Following the incident, dozens of other copycat acts were prevented by school authorities around the country. One week after the Colorado shootings, one student shot and killed another at a school in Canada.

The Second Amendment

Access to guns is a key controversy in this country. Many of the arguments between gun advocates and those who want to limit gun ownership, as well as between hunters and nonhunters, stem from how the Second Amendment to the Constitution of the United States is read and interpreted. The Second Amendment, which was ratified in 1791, reads: "A well regulated Militia, being necessary to the security of a free State, the right of the people to keep and bear Arms, shall not be infringed." Gun advocates read these words as illustrating a belief by the Founding Fathers that all Americans have the right to own guns. Gun control advocates read these same words and believe that the Founding Fathers intended to arm state militias to protect the young United States from attack, not to endorse gun ownership as a right of citizenship.

There are between 225 and 250 million privately owned guns in the United States, about the same number as there are people. Americans own four

After the American Revolution, the Founding Fathers wrote the Constitution of the United States. The Second Amendment concludes: ". . . the right of the people to keep and bear Arms, shall not be infringed."

times as many guns as they do dogs, three times as many guns as cats, nearly twice as many guns as cars, and about the same number of guns as television sets.[10] Guns caused 36,000 deaths in the United States in 1995. Half of these were suicides. Those who oppose gun ownership argue that it makes murder too easy. Half of the Americans murdered in 1995 were shot by a relative or friend or lover. As George Akerloff of the Brookings Institute said, "most murders occur because somebody got angry. . . . And if guns weren't available at the time, those murders would not have taken place."[11]

The United States has a death rate from guns that is nineteen times higher than that of any other industrialized nation. Other nations view America's liberal gun policy as somewhat difficult to understand. After the Jonesboro, Arkansas, murders, an Australian political scientist commented, "What's striking to people in other countries is what a tolerance there is in the U.S. for these scores of gun deaths."[12] The answer lies partly in the country's frontier heritage and in gunowners' use of the Second Amendment to the Bill of Rights.

The National Rifle Association, with its membership of 3 million people, strongly opposes any limits on gun ownership. Under the leadership of its president, movie actor Charlton Heston, the NRA has taken an even more aggressive stand against all forms of gun control. Heston believes that "of all our freedoms, the Second Amendment is first among equals. It is the one freedom that allows others to exist at all."[13]

Those who oppose gun control, such as Charlton Heston, base their argument on the language of the Second Amendment, maintaining that it guarantees citizens' right to own whatever guns they choose. Often they equate gun control with attacks on America's hunting heritage. The NRA Web site warns: "Our hunting heritage is under attack by uninformed, misguided people who wish to impose their values on society by any means possible."[14] This is similar to the theme of Heston's advertisements against gun control legislation: "There's a cultural war raging across America. Anti-gun media, politicians, educators and thought police are storming your values."[15]

Like the NRA and its supporters, many gun control advocates link guns with hunting. John Cullen, responding to an online discussion of the Second Amendment, wrote, "the reason we have [guns] is because we have a long tradition of hunting and gun ownership, not because it's part of our Constitutional heritage."[16]

The NRA energetically courts hunters. It celebrates hunters and hunting through its special Hunter Services Division. The Web site for this branch of the NRA claims, "Along with approximately 17 million American hunters and many national conservation organizations, we're working to preserve the American hunting tradition for future generations."[17] Because only 3 million people belong to the NRA and because there is no evidence that they are all hunters, the link between the NRA and hunters is weaker than the NRA would like. Most observers estimate that only 12.5 percent of all hunters are NRA members.

Most hunters are concerned about gun safety, support hunter education programs, and join with the millions of Americans who want to see mandatory childproof locks on firearms. They have no need for military assault weapons. As President Clinton stated, "You do not need an Uzi to go hunting."[18] Hunter and West Point graduate Lucian K. Truscott IV commented in an editorial on Clinton's proposed ban on a wide variety of assault weapons that "the culture of guns has changed [since I was a

Hunters argue that it is healthier and more natural for children to see where their meat comes from. They believe that killing for food is natural.

thirteen-year-old hunting with a sixteen-gauge shotgun]. . . . The NRA spends millions of dollars to lobby against laws that stipulate mandatory gun-safety courses or that create a system to license guns the same way we license cars . . . [and are] encouraging an irresponsible gun culture that supplants responsible gun ownership."[19] The kind of military assault weapons that the NRA is protecting and the gun control advocates hope to outlaw are specifically designed to kill people. One weapon was advertised in *Guns and Ammo* magazine as "good enough for a head shot at 100 yards or a body shot at 150 yards."[20] One of the young Jonesboro, Arkansas, boys charged with killing his classmates not only had hunted with his father, but had attended practical shooting courses with him. At these shooting ranges, pop-up human cutouts are the targets, not deer or ducks or elk.

Gun control and violence are very much on the minds of American citizens. A recent poll by *Seventeen* magazine found that 45 percent of teenagers felt they were in real danger from gun violence. Given this climate of fear, when organizations like the NRA connect hunting to guns, opponents of hunting are likely to gain supporters. The NRA has been losing membership over the past decade, although it hopes that Charlton Heston's Hollywood star appeal will attract new followers to the group. The more extreme the positions on gun control taken by groups such as the NRA, the more difficult it is for hunters to make the case for their gun ownership. As hunter David Petersen warned, if hunting is to continue in America, hunters must avoid "alignment with the no-compromise anti-environmental far-right radical militia mentality"[21] that opposes all gun control. The NRA was forced to cut back its annual meeting in Denver, Colorado, following the Columbine High School massacre in Littleton in 1999.

Hunters can help their cause in important ways. They can accept the need for more gun safety legislation, such as requiring childproof locks on guns, placing additional bans on automatic weapons, and mandating longer, more comprehensive hunter safety courses. These changes, authorities believe, would lower death rates and still permit hunting to exist.

6

The Pros and Cons of Hunting

As the United States enters the twenty-first century, it remains unclear whether hunting will continue, at least on public land. Private hunting, on individual farms and ranches, tracts of land owned by hunting clubs, and commercial preserves will probably continue to exist because Americans value private land ownership and free enterprise.

Many decisions about hunting will be made in the first quarter of the twenty-first century, and young people who are in middle school and high school today may well cast some of the votes that determine public policy.

Animal Population Growth and Habitat Reduction

For the most part, the wild game targeted by hunters depends on large tracts of undeveloped land and distance away from human beings. As the population of the United States continues to grow, more land will be overtaken by the needs of humans.

Whether they are hunters or nonhunters, all Americans need to think about ways to provide a stable habitat for wild animals. If hunting is discontinued, a major revenue source for wildlife management is also going to end. New taxes—or other sources of revenue—will have to be developed to preserve the animals' habitats.

Those who favor hunting and would like the percentage of hunters in the population to grow need to think seriously about the number of hunters per square mile that the nation's shrinking wild habitat can accommodate. Hunters and their allies also have to consider carefully the number and kinds of improvements they want to see in public hunting lands. For example, hunters often lobby for roads through public wildlife refuges. Although these may be convenient in the short run, they invite the development and use of modern technology that will destroy the natural character of the habitat. Technological improvements in refuge areas that make hunting more comfortable also give support to opponents' criticism that hunting is no longer a sport requiring wilderness skills.

The destruction of habitat is probably the most

serious threat facing animals and the hunting tradition today. As the hunting historian Charles Waterman predicted, "There are more and more hunters using less and less land."[1]

Hunting's American Tradition and Heritage

There is no question that hunting is an American tradition that dates back to the nation's earliest settlers. However, there are many aspects of colonial culture that are no longer valued in modern America: slavery, white male supremacy, exploitation of natural resources, dueling, and the oppression of American Indians, to name a few. Americans in the twenty-first century will need to decide whether hunting is a tradition that should be preserved or a tradition out of step with modern values.

Animal Rights

Over the last thirty years, the animal rights movement has heightened everyone's awareness of cruelty to animals. Whether or not hunting belongs in the category of cruelty to animals remains to be determined. If people continue to be meat eaters as they have been for thousands of years, animals will inevitably die. The question is then the following: Which is worse for these animals—to die by hunters' bullets and arrows, or to die in the slaughterhouse?

A growing minority of Americans would abolish all hunting. If they are successful, they must present a plan and pay for the maintenance of a stable, adequately fed wild animal population.

Both hunters and antihunters claim special regard for animals. Legislation about hunting in the next century will have to address the central issue of whether or not animals' rights are similar to or vastly different from the rights exercised by human beings.

Hunting and Conservation

Almost no one questions the role that hunters have played in the conservation of the major wild animals that are their targets.

If hunters are to maintain their reputation as conservationists, they must guard against the use of weaponry, vehicles, and hunting aids that hurt, rather than help, conservation efforts.

Hunting and Gun Control

Death from firearms, whether intentional or unintentional, is on the rise, particularly among children. Although a number of hunters use bow and arrow, most use guns. If hunting is to survive, hunters need to think carefully about gun control legislation, they must support responsible licensing and safety courses, and they must be committed to keeping firearms out of the hands of minors.

At the same time, those who oppose hunting are unfair if they assume that all hunters collect assault weapons, oppose any controls on their ownership, and spend their recreational hours shooting at fake human targets. Opponents of hunting could consider the European experience, in which hunting and gun control coexist.

Hunters have played a large role in the conservation of animals and their habitats, but if hunting is to survive, hunters must think carefully about gun control legislation.

An Emotional Issue

Hunting is an emotional issue for many Americans. It often touches family memories, enjoyment of the outdoors, love for animals, our national self-image and heritage, good times and bad times, and America's capacity for violence and injury to children. Both those who actively support hunting and those who oppose it play on our emotions in their appeals for support. In making your decision about hunting, it is important that you weigh the issues that have been presented in this book and that you do further research so that no matter what conclusion you reach, you know that you have made an intelligent, informed decision.

For More Information and Internet Addresses

Conservation Groups That Do Not Oppose Hunting

Defenders of Wildlife
1101 Fourteenth Street, NW
#1400
Washington, DC 20005
<http://www.defenders.org>

Izaak Walton League
707 Conservation Lane
Gaithersburg, MD 20878
<http://www.iwla.org>

National Audubon Society
700 Broadway
New York, NY 10003
<http://www.audubon.org>

Sierra Club
85 Second Street
Second Floor
San Francisco, CA 94105-3441
<http://www.sierraclub.org>

Wilderness Society
900 Seventeenth Street, NW
Washington, DC 20006-2506
<http://www.wilderness.org>

World Wildlife Fund
1250 Twenty-fourth Street NW
Washington, DC 20037
<http://www.panda.org>

Groups that Actively Promote Hunting

Boone and Crockett Club
250 Station Drive
Missoula, MT 59801
<http://www.boone-crockett.org>

Ducks Unlimited
One Waterfowl Way
Memphis, TN 38120
<http://www.ducks.org>

Foundation for North American Wild Sheep
720 Allen Avenue
Cody, WY 82414-3412
<http://www.iigi.com/os/non/fnaws/wheel.htm>

National Hunters Association
P.O. Box 16
Eagle Rock, NC 27523

National Rifle Association
Hunter Services Department
1600 Rhode Island Avenue, NW
Washington, DC 20036
<http://www.nra.org>

National Wildlife Federation
8925 Leesburg Pike
Vienna, VA 22184
<http://www.nwf.org>

Pheasants Forever
1783 Buerkle Circle
St. Paul, MN 55110
<http://www.pheasantsforever.org>

Quail Unlimited
31 Quail Run
Edgefield, SC 29824
<http://www.quailunlimited.org>

Rocky Mountain Elk Foundation
2291 West Broadway
Missoula, MT 59801
<http://www.rmef.org>

Whitetails Unlimited
P.O. Box 720
1715 Rhode Island Street
Sturgeon Bay, WI 54235
<http://www.whitetailsunlimited.org>

Groups that Actively Oppose Hunting

Alliance for Animals
122 State Street
#605
Madison, WS 53703
<http://www.allanimals.org>

American Anti-vivisection Society
801 Old York Rd.
#204
Jenkintown, PA 19046-1685
<http://www.aavs.org>

Committee to Abolish Sport Hunting
P.O. Box 562
New Paltz, NY 12561
<http://all-creatures.org/cash>

The Fund for Animals, Inc.
200 West Fifty-seventh Street
New York, NY 10019
<http://www.fund.org>

The Humane Society of the United States
2100 L Street NW
Washington, DC 20037
<http://www.hsus.org>

International Society for Animal Rights
421 South State Street
Clark's Summit, PA 18411

People for the Ethical Treatment of Animals
501 Front Street
Norfolk, VA 23510
<http://www.peta-online.org>

Chapter Notes

Chapter 1. A Dual Image—Heroes and Villains

1. James A. Swan, *In Defense of Hunting* (San Francisco: HarperSanFrancisco, 1995), p. 133.

2. T. H. Watkins, "The Wild and the Unwild," *Audubon*, March–April 1997, p. 128.

3. Ibid.

4. Swan, p. 121.

Chapter 2. Hunting: Who, What, and How?

1. Quoted in James A. Swan, *In Defense of Hunting* (San Francisco: HarperSanFrancisco, 1995), p. 190.

2. Stephen Kellert, "Attitudes and Characteristics of Hunters and Anti-Hunters," Transactions of the Forty-third North American Wildlife and Natural Resources Conference, 1978.

3. Erich Fromm, *The Anatomy of Human Destructiveness* (New York: Holt, Rinehart and Winston, 1973), p. 132.

4. Richard K. Nelson, "Introduction: Finding Common Ground," in David Petersen, ed., *A Hunter's Heart: Honest Essays on Blood Sport* (New York: Henry Holt and Company, 1996), p. 7.

5. John G. Mitchell, "Moose and Mongamoonga," in Petersen, p. 27.

6. Russell Chatham, "Dust to Dust," in Petersen, p. 269.

7. Swan, p. 248.

8. Robert Jackson, Robert Norton, and Raymond Anderson at the University of Wisconsin, cited in Ted Kerasote, *Bloodties: Nature, Culture and the Hunt* (New York: Kodansha International, 1994), p. 212.

9. Thomas McIntyre, *The Way of the Hunter: The Art and Spirit of Modern Hunting* (New York: E. P. Dutton, Inc., 1988), p. 8.

10. Ibid., pp. 8–9.

11. Kerasote, p. 213.

12. Richard Nelson, "Heart and Blood: Living With Deer in America," in Petersen, p. 219.

13. Kerasote, p. 215.

14. Charles F. Waterman, *The Hunter's World* (New York: Random House, 1982), p. 12.

15. Ibid.

16. "Techno Hunter," *The New York Times Magazine*, November 30, 1997, p. 114.

17. Frank Miniter, "Wingbone Turkey Call," *Outdoor Life*, April 1998, p. 98.

18. Ibid., p. 84.

19. Petersen, p. 157.

20. Advertisement, *Outdoor Life*, April 1998, p. 84.

21. *Cabela's*, Christmas 1997 catalog.

22. *Hunting*, fall 1997 catalog, p. 43.

23. *Deer*, fall 1997 catalog, p. 99.

Chapter 3. The Legacy of Hunting versus Animal Rights Activism

1. John Smith, "The Description of New England," reprinted in *American Literature* (Englewood Cliffs, N.J.: Prentice Hall, 1991), pp. 26–27.

2. Theodore Roosevelt, *The Wilderness Hunter: An Account of the Big Game of the U.S. and Its Chase with Horse, Hound and Rifle* (New York: G. P. Putnam's Sons, 1893), pp. 5–6.

3. Ibid., p. 8.

4. Ibid., p. 7.

5. Some American Indians, the Miwok, for example, were such expert swimmers that they could come up under a swimming duck and capture it by pulling it underwater by its feet.

6. Thomas McIntyre, "What the Hunter Knows," in David Petersen, ed., *A Hunter's Heart: Honest Essays on Blood Sport* (New York: Henry Holt and Company, 1996), p. 174.

7. A list of animal rights and hunting groups can be found in the For More Information and Internet Addresses section on p. 102 of this book.

8. James A. Swan, *In Defense of Hunting* (San Francisco: HarperSanFrancisco, 1995), p. 116.

9. Carl Cohen, "The Case Against Animal Rights," *Rohr*, Ibid., p. 25.

10. Ibid., p. 28.

11. Quoted in Swan, p. 48.

12. Swan, p. 191.

13. Jimmy Carter, "A Childhood Outdoors," in Petersen, p. 41.

14. Richard K. Nelson, "Finding Common Ground," in Petersen, p. 3.

15. Quoted in Charles S. Clifton, "The Hunter's Eucharist," in Petersen, p. 147.

16. Thomas McIntyre, *The Way of the Hunter: The Art and the Spirit of Modern Hunting* (New York: E. P. Dutton, 1988), p. 176.

17. Gail Shaffer, "Children and the Animal rights Agenda," *Field and Stream*, August 1995, p. 56.

18. PETA Web site, June 1998, <http://www.peta_online.org>.

Chapter 4. Hunting and Conservation

1. *The Hunter in Conservation* (Newtown, Conn.: The Council for Wildlife Conservation and Education, Inc., 1992), p. 24.

2. James A. Swan, *In Defense of Hunting* (San Francisco: HarperSanFrancisco, 1995), p. 7.

3. *The Hunter in Conservation*, p. 38.

4. The slang term *buck* meaning a one-dollar bill, derives from the fact that a deerskin sold for one dollar before the Civil War.

5. "National Hunting and Fishing Day" advertisement, *Hamilton County News*, September 23, 1997, p. 13.

6. Ted Kerasote, *Bloodties: Nature, Culture and the Hunt* (New York: Kodansha International, 1994), p. 232.

7. Ibid., p. 240.

8. Quoted in Richard Nelson, *Heart and Blood: Living with Deer in America* (New York: Alfred A. Knopf, 1997), p. 24.

9. Ibid., p. 309.

Chapter 5. Hunting and Gun Control

1. James A. Swan, *In Defense of Hunting* (San Francisco: HarperSanFrancisco), p. 169.

2. Ibid., p. 195.

3. Violence Policy Center, July 10, 1998, <http://www.vpc.org>.

4. Carmen Napolitano, "Hunters Take to the Woods to Bag the Coveted Whitetail," *Troy Record*, November 18, 1997, p. A1.

5. "First Week of Southern Zone Deer Season Safest Ever," *Troy Record*, November 28, 1997, p. B3.

6. Swan, p. 161.

7. Ibid.

8. "Witnesses Recount Shooting at High School in Mississippi," *The New York Times*, June 11, 1998, p. A28.

9. July 5, 1998, <http://www.ceasefire.html>.

10. Jackie Cooperman, "Kids Can Easily Get Guns," December 5, 1997, <http://abcnews.com>.

11. Jorgen Wouters, "The Land of Guns and Death," June, 30, 1998, <http://abcnews.com>.

12. Ibid.

13. NRA advertisement, *Outdoor Life*, summer 1998, p. 97.

14. Ibid.

15. NRA advertisement, *Outdoor Life*, April, 1998, p. 25.

16. Wouters, "The Land of Guns and Death."

17. NRA, May 30, 1998, <http://www.nra.or/hunter-svcs/fact.html>.

18. "A New Squeeze on Gun Imports," *The New York Times*, April 7, 1998, p. A26.

19. Lucian K. Truscott IV, "A Right to Bear 50 Assault Weapons," *The New York Times*, April 7, 1998, p. A27.

20. Ibid.

21. David Petersen, ed., *A Hunter's Heart: Honest Essays on Blood Sport* (New York: Holt, Rinehart and Winston, 1996) p. 156.

Chapter 6. The Pros and Cons of Hunting

1. Richard L. Worsnop, "Hunting Controversy," *Congressional Quarterly*, January 24, 1992, p. 67.

Further Reading

Clagget, Hilary D., ed. *Wildlife Conservation*. New York: H. W. Wilson, Co., 1997.

Hanson, Freya Ottem. *The Second Amendment: The Right to Own Guns*. Springfield, N.J.: Enslow Publishers, Inc., 1998.

Kerasote, Ted. *Bloodties: Nature, Culture and the Hunt*. New York: Kodansha International, 1993.

Mann, Charles C., and Mark L. Plummer. *Noah's Choice: The Future of Endangered Species*. New York: Alfred A. Knopf, Inc., 1995.

McIntyre, Thomas. *The Way of the Hunter: The Art and the Spirit of Modern Hunting*. New York: E. P. Dutton, 1988.

Nelson, Richard. *Heart and Blood: Living with Deer in America*. New York: Alfred A. Knopf, Inc., 1997.

Newton, David E. *Hunting*. Danbury, Conn.: Franklin Watts, Inc., 1992.

Petersen, David, ed. *A Hunter's Heart: Honest Essays on Blood Sport*. New York: Henry Holt and Company, 1996.

Roosevelt, Theodore. *The Wilderness Hunter: An Account of the Big Game of the U.S. and Its Chase with Horse, Hound and Rifle*. New York: G. P. Putnam's Sons, 1893.

Stange, Mary Zeiss. *Woman the Hunter*. Boston: Beacon Press, 1997.

Swan, James A. *In Defense of Hunting*. San Francisco: HarperSanFrancisco, 1995.

Index